MW00774930

# THE LITTLE BOOK OF
# LIFE HACKS

Copyright © 2024 Headline Publishing Group

The right of Katie Meegan to be identified as the Author of the Work has been
asserted by her in accordance with the Copyright, Designs and Patents Act 1988.

First published in 2024 by OH
An Imprint of HEADLINE PUBLISHING GROUP

2 4 6 8 10 9 7 5 3 1

**Disclaimer:**

All trademarks, copyright, quotations, company names, registered names,
products, characters, logos and catchphrases used or cited in this book are
the property of their respective owners.

Apart from any use permitted under UK copyright law, this publication may only
be reproduced, stored, or transmitted, in any form, or by any means, with prior
permission in writing of the publishers or, in the case of reprographic production, in
accordance with the terms of licences issued by the Copyright Licensing Agency.

Cataloguing in Publication Data is available from the British Library

ISBN 978-1-80069-634-1

Compiled and written by: Katie Meegan
Editorial: Saneaah Muhammad
Designed and typeset in Queulat by: Tony Seddon
Project manager: Russell Porter
Production: Arlene Lestrade
Printed and bound in Dubai

Headline's policy is to use papers that are natural,
renewable and recyclable products and made from
wood grown in well-managed forests and other
controlled sources. The logging and manufacturing
processes are expected to conform to the
environmental regulations of the country of origin.

HEADLINE PUBLISHING GROUP
An Hachette UK Company
Carmelite House, 50 Victoria Embankment, London EC4Y 0DZ

www.headline.co.uk    www.hachette.co.uk

THE LITTLE BOOK OF

# LIFE HACKS

## TIPS, TRICKS & SIMPLE WINS

FOR AN EASIER LIFE

# CONTENTS

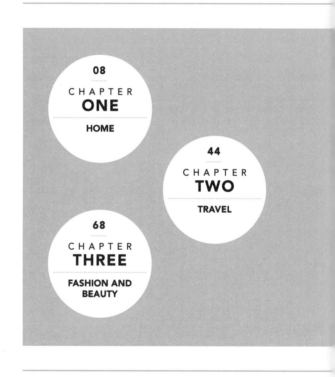

# INTRODUCTION

Welcome to *The Little Book of Life Hacks*!

Let's face it, life is busy. Don't you just wish there was an easier way to juggle work, family, school, friends and home? Well now there is!

In *The Little Book of Life Hacks*, you'll find a treasure trove of ingenious tips and tricks to streamline your life, covering everything from organizing your home and stress-free travelling to beauty and fashion shortcuts, savvy money management, maximising work productivity and even enhancing your culinary adventures. Trust us when we say, you'll wonder how you lived without them before!

We've trawled the internet to curate the best collection of life hacks you'll ever need. We can guarantee that hacking your day-to-day routines will make your life smoother, more efficient and, dare we say, more enjoyable! Whether you're looking to declutter your living space, master the art of packing light, achieve that perfect capsule wardrobe or even save a few bucks while grocery shopping, we've got you covered.

So, dive in and let these practical solutions empower you to reclaim your time and energy for the things that truly matter.

Let's hack life together!

CHAPTER
**ONE**

# HOME

Make your space your
sanctuary with these great
life hacks.

Whether it's decluttering,
cleaning or making the most of
your room, we've got you
covered with these homely
life hacks!

Are you sick of the annoying scratching when trying to find the end of the sticky tape?

Use a hairpin to mark the end of the tape so you have easy access the next time you need it!

To get rid of scratches or dings on furniture rub a walnut on it.

**Yes, a real walnut.**

It really works!

After washing and drying, stretch out the short ends of your towels.

This prevents cinching and makes towels last much longer.

## Who doesn't love a fluffy pillow?

If you have a dryer, pop your pillows in for a mere 10 minutes to help restore their delightful fluffiness.

# Have you got a cat who likes to scratch your couch to bits?

Use a beard trimmer to remove the excess cat-scratch threads and restore your furniture to its pre-kitty glory.

A family home is crazy enough without a million half-used cups and glasses everywhere!

Use coloured rubber bands to mark everyone's glass/ cup for the day (one per colour per family member), cutting down on that pesky washing up.

# Top Trash Tip No. 1

To make fitting a new garbage bag as easy as possible, first smooth the bag into a long tube, then simply drop it into your garbage bin.

Fold the top over the bin's edge, and you're good to go!

# Top Trash Tip No.2

Use a bungee cord to keep the garbage bag from slipping into the bin and creating more mess.

To fix the folded, curling
corner of a rug, place
a glass filled with cold
water on said corner and
surround it with ice cubes.

Give the ice cubes time
to melt, remove the glass
and voilà!

# Hate smashing your fingers with a hammer?

Silly question.

Use a pair of pliers to hold small nails in place when hammering to lower the chance of smashing your fingers. . .
and excessive swearing.

# Did you know...

The loops on the edge of a wire dish-drying rack are actually for holding tall glasses?

**Well now you do!**

## Difficult stains on your stovetop?

Spray some oven cleaner on the stains, give it a quick wipe and then cover the stove with plastic wrap (cling film) for the night.

In the morning just wipe and go!

# Write notes on your washing machine... yes really!

Use a dry erase marker to add notes to the surface of your machine, such as reminders to load the whites or not to shrink your favourite sweater in the dryer.

If you're lucky enough to have a garden, you'll know that there are lots of long-handled tools involved in maintaining your lush habitat.

Stop tripping over those tools by using a spare pallet to create a handy tool organizer!

### How?
Attach the pallet to a fence, shed or to the exposed wall studs in your garage, then simply slot your tools inside the pallets for easy access.

Reusable shopping bags are great for the environment, but maybe not so great for your sanity when the bottom rips open, spilling your milk and eggs onto the street.

To prevent undue ripping, add a small piece of plywood or sturdy cardboard to the bottom of the bag.

This is far sturdier than the plastic that usually comes with these bags, helping to distribute the weight of your groceries and avoid crying over spilt milk!

# Sick of your bathroom drawers being disorganized and generally chaotic?

Well, seek inspiration from elsewhere in the house – namely the kitchen.

Use a cutlery drawer organizer in the bathroom to keep all your little bottles in one tidy place. Not only are the compartments the perfect size for toothbrushes and toothpastes but it's also ideal for corralling lipsticks, razors, floss and more.

# Two more words for bathroom organization.
# Use. Magnets.
## You read that right!

Use super glue, or double-sided tape, to stick a few magnets to the back of the bathroom cabinet or inside the cabinet door. This is a very handy way to easily see and store metal self-care items like tweezers, scissors and nail clippers.

# File holders for kitchen organization?

## Are you mad?

Nope! Cheap and accessible, file holders are the perfect way to store a whole load of kitchen items, from cleaning items to chopping boards and placemats.

# Condiments becoming a nuisance?

Fortunately, the answer to tidying those wayward bottles is just a recycling bin away...

Keep your condiments under control by using an empty six-pack beer holder!

It's also a handy way to transport them to a BBQ or a picnic.

## Always losing your hair ties?

Use a carabiner to keep them all in one place. Bonus point for hanging your hair tie carabiner in a high place!

# Don't throw away your finished toilet roll tube!

Make your wrapping paper last even longer by making your own handy storage holder.

## How?

Simply cut an empty toilet paper tube lengthwise and wrap it around the roll of wrapping paper. Cinch up the tube as tight as possible, secure it in place with a piece of tape and hey presto!

An easily removable holder for the next time you need to wrap something.

# Do you have an empty wine box lying around?

Hey, we're not here to judge! But here's a tip... use the discarded wine box to store shoes. The cardboard dividers and sturdy box are perfect for keeping all your kicks in one place.

You can even get fancy with it! Paint the box or cover in wrapping paper and keep it by your front door.

# Remember that CD holder from the 90s?

Give it a new lease of life in the kitchen!

These outdated organizers are ideal for storing plastic container and pot lids.

# No space for a dry erase message board?

Why use an entire wall when you can use a picture frame!

Grab an unused frame and some paper, cut the paper to fit the frame and set it in behind the glass. Use a dry erase marker on the glass and voilà, you have the perfect way to leave messages!

# Hanging shoe organizers are far too versatile to be left in the closet.

Use them for storing gloves, accessories and jewellery.

Why stop in the bedroom?

You can even use them in the kitchen to store boxed and canned goods!

# Cut down on your single-use plastic consumption by storing plastic bags for later use.

But how to do this without leaving them in an unattractive pile?

By using a paper towel tube!
Easy to store, even easier to access.

# Too much clutter driving you mad?

This is one that is especially relevant to families:
**give everyone's items their own space.**

Label a container for each person in an entryway or a front hall. Frees up mess and it may even give your kids a reason to tidy up!

## Towel racks: they're not just for the bathroom.

Use an over-the-door hanger on the back of a closet door to create extra storage for tablecloths, bed sheets or blankets.

# Got some old bowls and a junk drawer?

Kill two birds with one stone by using old bowls and dishes to finally sort out that messy drawer.

Simply place a non-slip matt underneath and get organized!

## Stop making a dog's dinner of, well, your dog's dinner!

Instead of scooping pet food out of a precariously floppy bag, transfer the dry food into a sturdy lidded bin. Add a scooper and maybe give it a lick of paint to brighten up the outside!

# When it comes to organizing sponges and scrubbers, look up and over!

The sides of kitchen cupboards are usually underutilized and can make for great storage.

Get a small wire office organizer and hook it over the cupboard door, clearing valuable counter space.

# Sick of having a million different cables and cords and forgetting what they're for?

## Label them using bread tabs.

Plastic bread tabs are perfect because they're sturdy, have just enough room to write on and can even come in different colours!

# Too many wires covering your bedroom floor?

## Use a claw clip
to attach all your chargers
to your bed frame
and save some precious
floor space.

# Want your metals to shine?

**White vinegar**
is super versatile and can be used to clean just about anything in your home.

It's especially useful in getting limescale off shower screens and keeping chrome taps gleaming.

CHAPTER
**TWO**

# TRAVEL

Whether you're jetting off on an adventure to foreign lands or simply taking a weekend road trip, these travel tips are as essential as packing that passport!

# On the road again?

## Keep your car tidy with this handy hack!

Line a plastic cereal container with a bag to use as an in-car bin! To keep the bin from sliding around the car, apply a self-adhesive hook-and-loop fastener to the bottom of the container and stick it to your car's carpet.

## Use an old (but clean!) coffee cup as an in-car tissue holder.

Simply fill the cup with tissues, cut a slit in the lid, pull your tissues through and there you go!

Keep it in your cup holder to beat those sniffles on the go.

# Always getting your keys confused?

## Paint them with nail varnish!

Use a different colour for each key to help identify them in a secure manner, and cut down on all the doorway faff.

## This is one
## for the cyclists!

If you're sick of getting rain on your seat, get a shower cap. No, not for your head, for your bum.

A good-quality shower cap makes for a perfect bike seat cover, saving your trousers and your wallet.

# Are you travelling without a toothbrush container?

Use a water bottle
to protect those bristles!

## Staying somewhere with no laundry basket?

Tie the neck of a large hoodie to close the hole and turn it upside down; you now have an on-the-go laundry basket!

Plus, it makes it easier to pack and separate from your clean clothing.

## Luggage scales.

### Buy them.

They may seem like a bit of an investment at the time, but we can guarantee you that they're cheaper than ANY airline's excess baggage fees.

## If you're a frequent flyer, consider getting a travel credit card.

They're usually underwritten by major banks and can help you earn points and rewards towards your next trip.

Always make sure to do your research and check the T&Cs.

# Travel on a budget by cutting out accommodation costs!

There are so many ways to see the world without shelling out for hotels and resorts.

Websites such as Trusted Housesitters, Nomador, Couchsurfing and MindMyHouse offer low-cost and often free accommodation alternatives.

# Peak or off-peak?
## Go in-between!

If you have the flexibility, consider travelling during "shoulder season" – in Europe, this usually ranges from April to mid-June and September through to October.

Not only will you save money, but usually the weather is still warm and the beaches less crowded – ideal!

# You can never have too many...

Nowadays, it's so easy to have absolutely everything from boarding passes to hotel bookings on our phones.

However, there's no harm in keeping **paper copies** of essential information, juuuuust in case!

# Hola!

Even when going to a touristy area, it'll be useful to learn some **phrases in the local language.**

"Hello", "thank you", "how much is..." and "do you speak English" are just some basics that could help you out in most situations.

TRAVEL

# Did you know...

You can still use Google Maps when you have no internet.

Ahead of time, use the download feature to select a section from the map and save an offline version of the place you're visiting.

# Travelling to more than one country this year?

Consider getting a universal adapter – they're slightly more expensive than a single country adapter but they'll be worth it in the long run, trust us!

And if you simply have too many electronics when travelling to one place, consider taking an extension cord and one foreign adapter. You'll have multiple sockets, so your electronics won't be competing for juice!

# Too many clothes to fit in your carry-on bag?

Remove the inside of a neck pillow and instead fill it with any excess clothing.

Airlines must allow you to bring a neck pillow onboard, and you get to avoid the extra baggage fees.

**Win-win!**

# Use incognito mode on your internet browser when booking flights.

Airline sites often use tracking software to monitor your travel searches and may hike up the prices. Avoid this by going incognito to get the best deal.

# The Google Translate app has a camera feature.

Simply open and scan the text you wish to translate – no more accidentally ordering the most surprising thing on the menu!

# Is your suitcase about to burst?

Any experienced traveller will tell you that **packing cubes** are the way to go – they're a number one hack for a reason!

You can get them online or from many retailers.

# Are you a light sleeper?

If you're staying in a hotel, consider bringing some Blu Tack® with you.

Use small amounts to cover those annoying blinking red lights on TVs so you can get some decent shuteye.

## Planning a trip sometime soon?

Comparison sites like Skyscanner and Google Flights let you set up price alerts to get the best deal on flights!

# Put something heavy in your purse or wallet when in crowded tourist spots.

This makes your valuables more difficult to pickpocket as you'll instantly feel if something is off.

# Before being dissuaded by a one-star review, take a look at the reviewer's history by clicking on their profile.

If it's a one off, chances are they genuinely had a bad experience.

If they're a serial complainer, you might need to take that review with a pinch of salt.

CHAPTER
**THREE**

# FASHION AND BEAUTY

Whether you wear suits every day or live in the same pair of jeans you've had for years, your wardrobe can either be a source of daily comfort or an unnecessary hassle.

Take the confusion out of dressing with these life hacks – oh, and we have a few tips for skincare, too!

# Does clearing out your wardrobe feel like an endless struggle?

Designate a donation corner/box/bag and set a reminder to clear it out seasonally.

## Rotate your wardrobe and store seasonal items in vacuum bags.

Not only will this save your closet space, but each season will let you look at your clothing with fresh eyes, seeing what really needs to be refreshed, replaced or mended.

## Consider building a capsule wardrobe.

Ironically, paring back your options actually makes you feel like you've more choice in coordinating comfortable and fashionable outfits.

Use Pinterest boards to explore your style and take it from there.

## Too many clothes?

In order to keep your capsule wardrobe in great shape, follow the one-in-one-out rule. Simply put, for every new item you purchase, an old item goes in the donation box.

Not only does this keep your wardrobe fresh, but it also keeps it manageable!

# Falling off the rack...

To stop silky shirts and strappy tops slipping, wrap a few coils of pipe cleaners around the top of their hangers.

## Short on space or want to store similar items together?

Use a tab from a drinks can, slip it over the hook of a hanger until it reaches the neck and then hook another hanger through the second opening of the tab.

Voilà, double hangers!

## Protect delicate items while using old pillowcases.

Cut a small slit into the closed end of the pillowcase and pull the hook of the hanger through – instant clothing bag!

# Keep fleeces and plush clothing fluffy for longer by drying them in a pillowcase.

Quickly put the items in the pillowcase and tie it closed before tossing into the dryer. This protects the fibres from balling in the machine.

# Moving house?

Don't worry about taking all your clothes off their hangers.

Simply gather four or five already hanging items and wrap a bin bag around for easy transfer!

# Do you keep losing your favourite pair of earrings?

If you ever lose jewellery or other small items under furniture, put a stocking or a pair of tights over the nozzle of a vacuum and swipe it around the area where the item was lost.

The piece of jewellery will then get sucked onto the material, making it easily retrievable!

**Don't you just hate it when you know that there's more toothpaste in the tube, but it just won't come out?!**

We have a solution for you – break a chopstick in half, align each half to the bottom of the tube (on either side), secure the ends of the chopstick with rubber bands and push downwards – instant toothpaste!

## Need a helping hand?

If you're struggling to put on a bracelet with a clasp, use a small bit of tape to secure one end of the bracket to your wrist, freeing up the other hand to connect the clasp.

# Always losing hairpins?

Just use a large safety pin to keep them all in one place – also very handy for travelling!

## Uh oh...

You've ripped your tights...
but don't fear.

An oldie but a goodie – put
clear nail varnish on
tights to stop ladders from
developing further.

# Only have space for one cosmetic?

The most versatile piece of make-up you can own is a neutral/pink lipstick.

Not only can you use it for its intended purpose, but any decent lipstick can double as both blusher and eyeshadow – you're welcome!

# Wipe sunglasses, prescription glasses and your mobile phone daily with an alcohol wipe.

Not only does this help kill any bacteria on these well-used items but it also helps those with acne-prone skin avoid unnecessary breakouts where your glasses or phone sit.

# Too little sleep causing under-eye bags?

## This hack works every time!

Place two teaspoons in the freezer until they become cold and then hold them under each eye for 20 seconds to relax the blood vessels and reduce puffiness.

## Want to feel silky smooth?

When shaving intimate areas, opt for conditioner instead of shaving cream.

Not only does it give an incredibly smooth shave, but it even adds hydration to those sensitive zones.

It's also one less product to clutter your bathroom!

# From day to night...

For a liquid eyeliner that won't budge, ditch the actual eyeliner.

## Yes, really!

Instead, dip an eyeliner brush into waterproof mascara and draw directly onto your upper lash line. Just make sure you have a decent cleanser to get it off after!

# Greasy hair but out of dry shampoo?

## Use baby powder!

Just let it sit for a few minutes to absorb the excess oils then rub it around your scalp to get rid of the residuè.

# Looking for an all-natural makeup remover?

## Coconut oil is your go-to!

It's perfect for gently and effectively removing all traces of make-up, especially on sensitive skin.

However, we'd recommend following up with a cream-based cleanser if your skin tends to be on the oilier side.

# Want a natural glow without committing to fake tan?

Mix two parts foundation (a shade or two darker than your actual skin tone for that tanned effect) with one part liquid highlighter and a good dollop of lotion. Apply everywhere desired and leave a few minutes to dry.

Not only does it give you a lovely glow, but this mixture also smooths out imperfections and evens up skin tone!

## Public Service Announcement: STOP HANGING YOUR SWEATERS!

Seriously, gravity wreaks havoc with the natural shape of knitwear, causing them to stretch out over time in all the wrong places.

**Fold them. Now.**

# Out shopping and want to quickly see if a pair of trousers will fit you?

Hold both sides of the waistband in either hand and wrap it around your neck. If your hands don't touch or if your hands overlap, they're going to be too big or too small respectively.

Save yourself dressing room drama by narrowing your search down to trousers that will actually fit!

CHAPTER
**FOUR**

# WORK AND PRODUCTIVITY

It's all well and good life-hacking your space, but what about hacking your time?

Whether it's for work, school or to spend more time on your hobbies and side-hustles, embrace these productivity tips to get the most out of your day.

# Set your timers for tasks you've been putting off.

If you hate cleaning, set yourself a timer to clean or to declutter for 10 to 15 minutes. Sweeten the deal with yourself by sticking on your favourite podcast or an upbeat playlist.

If you live in an apartment building and receive a lot of packages, this is one for you.

## Put your apartment number on the bottom of your door for proof of delivery.

Most of the time, delivery drivers don't take a picture of the full door so it's difficult to confirm if it's yours and this eliminates the problem!

# When drafting an important email, add the recipient as the very, very last step!

This stops you from accidentally sending half-finished emails and having to repeat yourself or recall the message.

# Similarly, use the "Delay Send" option on emails.

Even if it's just for 15 minutes, this gives you time to correct any unintentional errors before it really reaches its intended destination.

## Phew!

# "... Hello?"

Easily spot scam calls from your mobile provider by immediately asking the caller if they know your name.

**If they don't, then it's a scam.**

Note: there are many other ways that scammers can trick you, so be sure to learn all the signs!

# If you're struggling to make a big decision, use the "two-day rule".

### How it works:

Give yourself two days. On the first day, pretend that you've made a choice in one direction, fully commit to it and explore all the feelings it brings up.
On the second day, do the same thing with the other option.

Try it out the next time you feel stuck on something and see if it works for you!

# Embrace the concept of time blocking.

Time blocking is a productivity method that divides your day into chunks of time. Each time block is then dedicated to accomplishing a specific goal.

This helps keep your attention on a singular task and saves you time in the long run.

## Have a seemingly endless to-do list?

Start each day by selecting the three most important tasks that you need to get done that day and focus solely on them.

Combine this with time blocking and really level up your productivity!

# Continuously distracted by the internet?

## Aren't we all.

Use website blockers to keep you off time-consuming sites and social media during focus time.

# Have a task that can be done in two minutes or less?

## Just do it, there and then.

This is the two-minute rule, and we guarantee that it'll take you less time to do it immediately instead of remembering to do it later.

# Make a playlist!

Studies have shown that listening to mood-enhancing music can increase productivity.

Over 78% of workers confirm that listening to music makes them more productive.[*]

Compose a playlist to keep you motivated and focused!

[*] As seen on Tracy Brower, "Music Enhances Productivity: The Science Behind The 10 Best Songs", forbes.com, December 10, 2023.

# Have regular tasks that keep cropping up throughout your workday?

Take some time to create templates to copy and paste to save you from repeating the same information over and over.

You'll thank yourself later!

# Have a seemingly endless to-do list and no way to prioritize?

Employ the Eisenhower matrix!

Divide a page into four boxes and label the top "Urgent" and "Not Urgent" and the sides "Important" and "Not Important".

Add your tasks to the relevant boxes and take the steps indicated.

|  | **Urgent** | **Not Urgent** |
|---|---|---|
| **Important** | **Do**<br>Do it now. | **Decide**<br>Schedule a time to do it. |
| **Not Important** | **Delegate**<br>Who can do it for you. | **Delete**<br>Eliminate it. |

# Take regular breaks using the Pomodoro Technique.

This requires breaking your day into smaller, more manageable chunks. Set a timer for 25 minutes and reward yourself with a five-minute break. After four chunks, take a longer 20-minute break.

(You can even use that time to say "pomodoro" over and over until it sounds funny!)

## If you can, try to work near natural light.

Being near natural light boosts mood and, as a result, productivity.

# If you have the freedom to do so in your job, try to divide your work into "theme days".

Day theming involves assigning specific days to specific types of work, e.g. Monday is for meetings, project work on Tuesdays, etc.

CEOs love it!

## Group similar tasks together to optimize your focus.

By grouping similar tasks together, such as sending several outstanding emails together, you avoid switching between tasks and feeling the negative effects of multitasking.

# Set specific times to check social media.

## Yes, really!

By giving yourself 10 minutes during the day to catch up on Instagram, TikTok or personal messages, you actually curb the impulse to continuously check in during the day.

Once you've caught up you can then switch your notifications back onto "Do Not Disturb" to continue with your work.

Just don't let your boss catch you doing it...

# Hack your workspace with colours!

Whether it's at home or in the office, add more red and blue into your environment. Studies have shown that red increases attention and blue sparks creativity.*

*"Effect of Colours: Blue Boosts Creativity, While Red Enhances Attention to Detail", *Science*, February 27, 2009.

# Have a massive project to complete that seems impossible?

Break it down into mini deadlines and milestones. Not only will it make the whole thing more manageable, but you can even reward yourself along the way!

# Did you know...

It's not groundbreaking news that exercise is good for you, but we'll bet you didn't know that the time of day you exercise can have massive knock-on effects throughout your day.

Moving in the morning spikes brain activity and prepares you to handle complex tasks. If you're not a morning person, working out in the middle of the day refreshes your brain for the afternoon.

# Getting constant messages from team members?

Use your calendar to block out dedicated focus time using the **"Do Not Disturb"** function.

# There's an app for that!

Get appy with your goals. There are lots of free apps that track your time and progress towards your goals. Pick one you like to break your goals down and keep you on track to great things.

You could even add a screen-time widget to your phone's home screen to keep track of your mobile usage.

# Leave your phone in another room.

## Yes, really.

A University of Texas study found that even having your phone in the same room decreases concentration, even if it's silent or in a bag.*
So hack your concentration by leaving it in another room.

*"The Mere Presence of Your Smartphone Reduces Brain Power, Study Shows", *Journal of the Association for Consumer Research*, April 3, 2017.

# Cut your email clutter.

Take some time to unsubscribe from spam, set up specific folders and generally tidy up your inbox. You can even set up two email addresses, one for friends and family or work and another for subscriptions, marketing and newsletters.

## Dirty laptop or computer screen?

If you can't get your hands on a standard microfibre cloth, use a clean coffee filter. It does a surprisingly good job!

# Hack your keyboard by learning shortcuts!

Here are some common ones to get you started:

## PC

**Alt + Tab:** switch between open programs

**Control + C:** copy

**Control + V:** paste

**Control + Z:** undo

## Mac

**Command + Tab:** switch between open programs

**Command + C:** copy

**Command + V:** paste

**Command + Z:** undo

CHAPTER
**FIVE**

# MONEY

Money, money, money – it makes the world go round. But does your bank balance make your head spin?

Try these financially savvy tips to save you that precious dough.

# Percentages

## Here's something they didn't teach you in school – how to quickly calculate percentages!

For example: what is 20% of 30?

Simply take the first number, so in this case 2 and multiply it by the first number of the second figure, so 3.

2 x 3 = 6
So, **6** is 20% of 30.

Another one:
What is 40% of 80?

4 x 8 = 32
So, the answer is **32.**

# Are your eyes bigger than your stomach?

Your mother was right, never ever do your groceries on an empty stomach, because you WILL end up buying more than you need.

# Takeaway?
# Nah, we already have dinner ready to go!

Not only does meal prepping hack your time and money, but it can help you become healthier too! We know that the idea of cooking for hours on end for the week ahead seems a bit boring but think of it this way:

One hour of cooking every day is saved. Ingredients are used. Money is saved.

## Actively commit to one or two spend-free/low-spend days a week.

You don't have to sit at home and stare at paint drying either, check out free amenities and events in your local area!

# Hold on, what's that?

Do a **subscription check**. You'll be amazed at how many things you've signed up for over the course of a year or two that you don't even use (or remember) anymore.

In fact, some companies actually rely on you forgetting to use them!

## Stay ahead of the game.

At least once a year, take a look at your **regular bills** and see if there's a way to get a better deal.

With some companies, all you need to do is ask or you can use trusted price comparison websites.

# Does your money seemingly disappear into thin air?

Being tap-happy might be a cause! Studies have shown that people are more careful with their money when they can see the, well, money!

Withdrawing a set amount of cash for daily expenses or cash-stuffing could be the way to go.

# Fancy a quick
# few bucks?

Sell what you no longer need! Apps like eBay, Depop and Vinted are great resources for selling unwanted clothing and household items.

# Round up your change!

Banking apps like Monzo and Revolut allow you to round up your expenses and increase your savings.

So, for example, if you spend £2.50 on a coffee, the app will round it up to £3 and pop the remaining 50p into your savings.

CHA-CHING!

# Go big or go home!

Most supermarkets have the price per unit printed under the actual price. Sometimes buying a slightly bigger packet of something actually gives you more value for money!

Or conversely, sometimes getting multiple smaller packets of an item might be the way to go. Use the price per unit to guide your decision making for better value.

# When it comes to getting value out of your clothing, opt for quality over quantity.

Three tops for $10 might seem like a good deal at the time, but spending $30 on one top that will last three times as long is actually saving you money in the long run.

# After getting those quality clothing pieces that will last you longer – get them tailored.

Not only does tailoring make you look smarter and make your clothes fit better, by fixing any small tears or frayed edges you'll also make your clothing last longer.

# There is a YouTube video for fixing everything.

## Yes, everything!

Before reaching for the phone to call a handyman, give it a go yourself (safely!) using YouTube.

If nothing else, it can then help you make an informed decision between attempting the task yourself and paying someone else to do it.

**Fancy going to a garage sale or doing a spot of thrift (charity) shop browsing?**

Go to affluent areas. The chances of finding a good quality bargain are quadrupled!

# Dust off that library card!

No longer are libraries just for books but most libraries now offer access to thousands of magazines, DVDs, eBooks and audiobooks.

## Look in the World Foods aisle for spices and other staples.

Chances are they'll be cheaper than their English-labelled counterparts in other aisles.

# If your feet are on the smaller side, check out the children's aisle for shoes.

Often the smaller adult sizes and larger youth sizes overlap.

**Bargain!**

## Not only are reusable water bottles good for the environment but they're good for your wallet too!

Save on buying drinks when out and about by keeping your bottle topped up from public fountains or coffee shops.

**Hydration is key!**

# At-home workouts!

We've all done it: bought the expensive gym membership in January only to stop going by March.

Save yourself the hassle by focusing on exercises that you can do at home!

There are loads of low-cost fitness apps with tons of classes or, if you don't want to spend money at all, YouTube also has loads of free videos.

# How to fix
# nearly any appliance
# yourself:

Find out the make/model.

Use YouTube and Google to
diagnose the problem.

Use an appliance-parts site to look at
the diagrams for each make/model and
figure out the part you need.

Order said part, either from the
appliance site or Amazon, or enter the
part number into Google.

Hop back on to YouTube to learn
how to install the part.

# Save yourself a trip to the garage by fixing minor dents and bumps yourself!

Pour hot water on the dent and lightly push it back into position from the inside. Keep those bumpers in tip-top condition!

# Another money- and environment-saving hack – reusable cups!

Most coffee shops now offer discounts for customers that bring their own travel mugs, saving coins and polar bears.

## Coupons, coupons, coupons!

On the website, in the paper, or even on the apps!

Use coupons to their full advantage to save money and get great deals.

## If you can, use online shopping for your weekly grocery shop.

Not only will it help you stick to your list by significantly cutting down on impulse buys, but it's a lot easier to spot deals... and use those precious coupons.

## Automate your savings to go into your account right after getting paid.

This will stop you from spending that money you were supposed to put away. It's also one less thing to think about!

## Try the baby aisle for cosmetic products such as cotton buds, sunscreen and earbuds.

This is a great option for those with sensitive skin – baby items are usually formulated with fewer chemicals, making them gentler on your skin.

# Save on electricity costs by switching to LED bulbs.

With over ten years of life, these smart bulbs will cut down on your electricity bill immediately.

## If you're the creative type, consider hand making gifts.

Not only will it bring the personal touch that the recipient will never forget but you might even discover a new hobby or possibly a side-hustle out of it!

CHAPTER
SIX

# FOOD

Did we save the best for last?
You decide!

Hack your kitchen skills
with these well-kept foodie
secrets. You'll be feeling like a
top chef in no time!

# Streamline your spice rack and get rid of all those half-empty glass bottles.

## How?

Use empty TicTac boxes for compact storage that is quickly accessible and easy to label.

## Eat your burger upside down!

Not only does this prevent the sauces and toppings from falling out, but the top bun is usually thicker than the bottom, absorbing more of the juicy sauces and flavours.

# Can't fit two pizzas on one oven tray?

## Try this.

Cut each pizza in half and turn the semicircles to face the outer edges of the oven tray.

## Perfecto!

## Multipurpose appliances!

Speaking of pizza cutters, they can be used for so much more than just cutting pizza.

Use them for ham or fresh herbs to make chopping hassle-free!

# Cold butter?
# Warm toast?

## No problem!

Use a cheese grater to shred a cold stick of butter over your toast of choice to make it easier to spread.

# Love iced coffee but hate the ice watering your coffee down?

## Who doesn't?

Get the best of both worlds by pouring cooled coffee into an ice tray and freezing.

For your quick coffee-fix, pop some coffee ice cubes into a cup with your milk of choice and be on your way. The coffee ice cube will eventually melt, giving you that tasty icy treat.

# To stop apple slices going bad, squeeze some lemon juice over them.

This stops them from oxidizing for a few days, giving you time to snack at will.

## Limited freezer space?

Give your frozen food boxes the Elsa treatment and let it go!

Pop your frozen items in plastic bags, cut out the cooking instructions, tape them to the bag and instantly reclaim freezer room!

# Use an old trouser hanger with clips to keep bags of crisps closed.

Perfect for picnics, days out or the beach.

## Store your freshly made fruit salad in a strainer inside a larger bowl.

This keeps the fruit just above their juices, which keeps them fresher for longer.

**Yum!**

# Did you know...

Spring onions keep growing after you've bought them. Yes, really!

Stick your spring onions in a jar and add some water. Change the water daily so they don't get soggy, trim off any dried or dead parts and voilà! Free infinite spring onions!

## Ice cream and movies?

Is there a more elite combination?

Serve your scoops in a wine tumbler to keep them frozen for longer.

# When eating an orange, hold the segments against the light to illuminate the pips.

## No more pip surprises!

## Love ice cream but hate the mess?

This one is perfect for kids, or for the messier eaters among us.

**In the summer, poke an ice lolly stick through a paper towel to catch any drips or spillages.**

# Wipe those tears...

Let's face it, no one enjoys **slicing onions**. So, here's what you're going to do:

Remove the outer layer, stab the onion with a fork to get a good purchase then slide a potato peeler back and forth to make thin cookable slices.

**You're welcome!**

# It's science!

If you ever have ketchup at the bottom of the bottle or some shampoo that you just can't get at, don't do the usual shaking up and down or slapping the bottle. Try this physics-inspired hack instead:

Put the cap back on and turn the bottle upside down.

Spin the bottle in a fast circular motion for five to ten seconds as if you're stirring a big pot of soup.

Open the cap and watch the liquid come out immediately!

# For perfectly stirred peanut butter, place the jar upside down in the fridge.

The oil rises naturally to the top of the peanut butter (or in this case the bottom of the jar), and the coldness of the fridge slows down the process ensuring perfectly mixed peanut butter every time!

# When reheating pasta in the microwave, put the sauce at the bottom of the bowl and then pour the pasta on top.

This stops the sauce from spitting all over your microwave and it heats more evenly!

# Use a plastic knife to cut brownies when they're still warm and relatively fresh out of the oven.

With the plastic knife you get far cleaner lines without the crumbled (and delicious) mess!

## Have a piece of toast that was left in the toaster for too long?

Toss in brown sugar, it'll soften right up and add some extra sweetness!

# Have a baguette or a whole loaf of bread that's about to go stale?

Quickly run the bottom of the bread under cold water and then place it into a preheated oven at 400°F/200°C for about 10 minutes.

It will come out as fresh and crispy as the day it was made!

## Stop crying over chopped onions!

Put your onion in the freezer for about 30 minutes before you chop it, which stops the release of the chemicals that sting your eyes.

No more tears!

# There's nothing worse than chopping a mango and the juice going absolutely everywhere!

Luckily, we have the solution for you. Simply chop the mango in half lengthways and use a clean glass to scoop out the flesh. Works every time!

## Have an avocado that's not yet ripe?

Store it in your fruit bowl next to the bananas to ripen it quicker.

Conversely, if you have an avocado that's about to go off, keep it well away from your bananas!

# Get more bang for your buck out of lemons and limes.

Before juicing, pop them in the microwave for seven to ten seconds, take them out and roll them back and forth over a countertop for ten more seconds.

For less than a minute's effort, you get a whole load more juice!

# Did you know...

## Honey has an infinite shelf life.

Even if your pot of honey is crystallized, this doesn't mean that it's gone off.

All you need to do is pop the jar in a bowl of hot water for five to ten minutes and it's as good as new.

## Anything to save the bees!

# Unsure if your eggs have gone off?

Put them to this eggs-cellent float test!

Simply pop your eggs in a bowl of water.

If they sink, they're okay to use. If they float, it's time to go.

## Ordered some fish and chips for dinner?

Stick a cup of water in the microwave along with your food. The steam created from the water stops the chips from drying out. Just make sure that your cup is microwave-proof and your chips are tasty!

# Eaten too much?

## This is the ultimate way to cure the hiccups!

While standing up, take a glass of water and put your mouth onto the furthest side, lower your head to the ground (as if you were going to touch your toes) and drink from the "wrong" side of the glass.

**It works, we swear!**

Get rid of those garlic and onion smells from your hands quickly and easily by rubbing your hands with baking powder or over stainless steel.

Lemon juice also works to neutralize garlic and onion smells – just make sure that you don't have any open cuts or broken skin on your hands first, cause that'll sting!

# Have some unripe pears?

Put them in a brown paper bag and leave in direct sunlight for a day, and it'll soften them right up!

# Who doesn't love garlic?

If you're mincing a large quantity of nature's finest flavour, add a pinch of salt to stop the garlicky goodness sticking to your knife or garlic press.

# Leftover sauce that's just simply too good to throw away?

Pour it into an ice cube tray and freeze! Once the sauce is frozen, transfer it over to freezer bags, making it easily accessible the next time you need it.

This also works for soups, broths and gravies!

## Filled to the brim?

To prevent water on the stove from boiling over and causing messes, lay a wooden spoon across the top of the pot.

**We don't know how, but it works!**

# Don't let your herbs go to waste!

If your fresh herbs are about to go off, chop them up, place them in an ice cube tray, pour over some water and oil and freeze.

The next time you need them for a dish simply grab them from your freezer and pop them in the pot!

## Made a batch of delicious cupcakes or muffins, only to realize that you don't have any cases?

Don't worry about running out to the shops, simply cut up some baking paper to line your tin instead!

# And lastly, here's a breakfast tip!

Making the perfect fried egg is no easy task, so here's what you're gonna do:

Before putting the pan over the heat, break your eggs into the pan. Then, add a good splash of water. Add your pan to the heat and cook slowly for picture-perfect eggs.